Fuzzy Stepbrothers

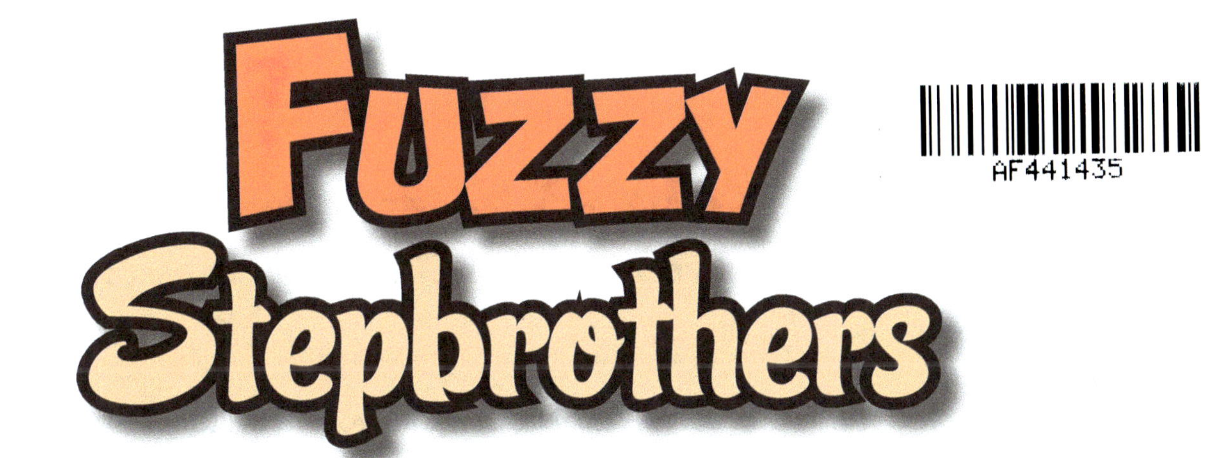

Short Stories of Shy Rescue Cats

Written By
Annette Morano

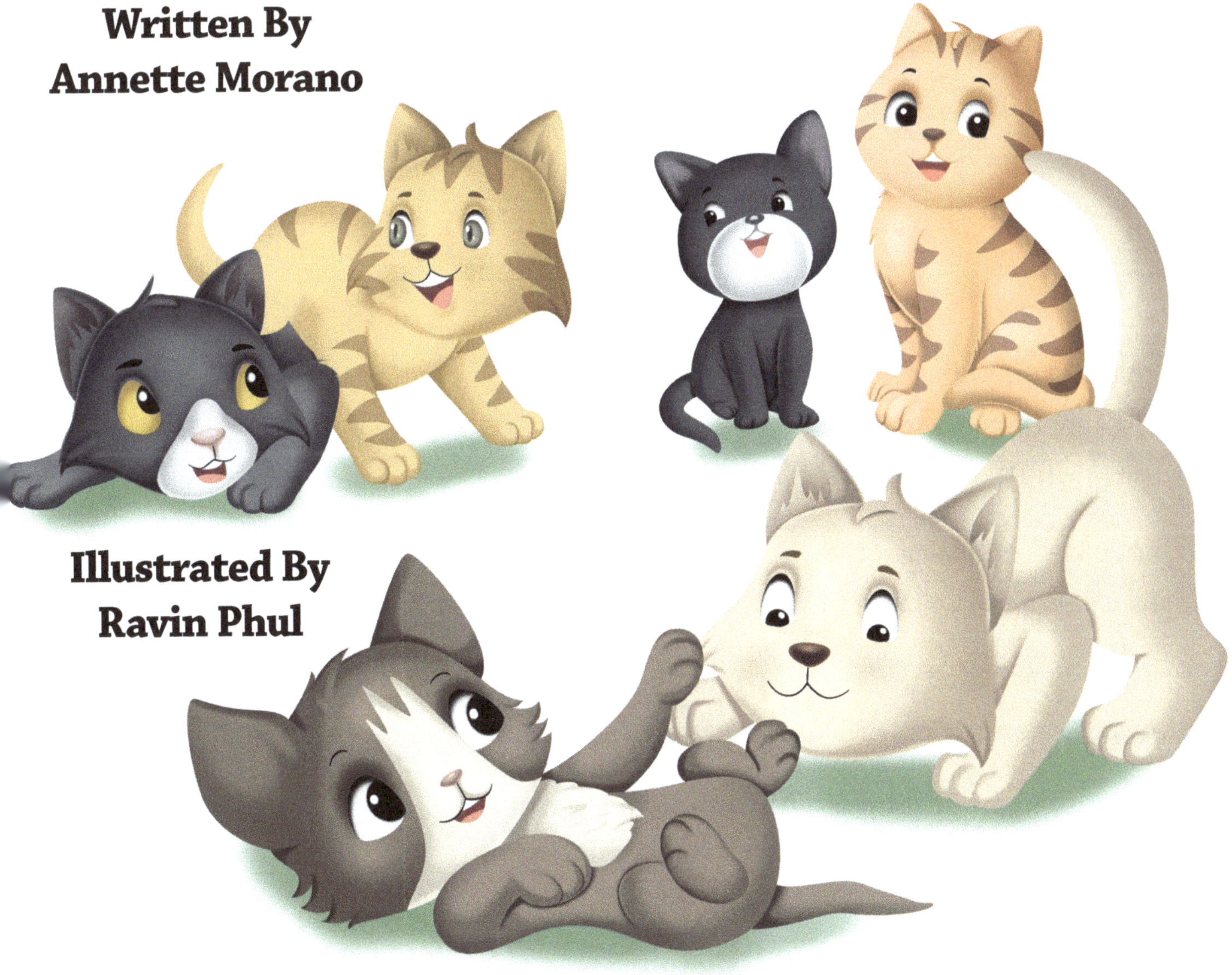

Illustrated By
Ravin Phul

This book is dedicated to Becky Weber, owner of Rebecca's Rescues. Becky has tirelessly done her best to save homeless cats and kittens for the past 14 years with the help of volunteers like myself.

It is recommended that an adult read this book to a young child. Then encourage that child when they start to read that they read it to their pet. A child reading to their pet promotes fluency, motivation and confidence. When a child reads to their pet, there is no judgment.

Fuzzy Stepbrothers

"Saving one cat will not change the world, but surely for that one cat, the world will change forever."

— Karen Davison

This edition was published in May 2024

Text by Annette Morano

Illustrations by Ravin Phul

ISBN: 9798323482368

Library of Congress Control No.: 2024905864

All inquiries can be sent by visiting the author's website @www.annettemoranobooks.com

Veronica, "Ronnie" for short, is sitting with her Mom. Oliver is curled up on the floor. He appears to be so bored and lonely. Ronnie says, "Mom, I think Oliver needs a friend." Mom agrees and they make a plan to go the next day to the animal shelter.

Ronnie and her Mom plan on getting a little kitten, but as they pass by the cages of the older animals, a paw reaches out through the cage to them. They hear a loud "meow." They turn and before them is a big, fat, orange cat. He seems to be talking to them and yearning to be held. They scoop him up and tell the women working there that they will take him enthusiastically.

Once they are back home, he meets his stepbrother, Oliver. At first Oliver isn't sure how he will feel about this stranger. He was expecting a little friend not a big, old cat.

That quickly changes after a few licks from Pumpkin. They call him "Pumpy" for short. They snuggle together for many long cat naps. Oliver soon can't imagine not having his stepbrother around.

After a few years, Ronnie notices Pumpy isn't quite right. He seems wobbly and skinnier than he used to be. He also has been drinking a lot of water. Ronnie tells Mom that they had better take him to the vet.

Pumpy is checked out by the friendly veterinarian and tells Ronnie that he has diabetes. This is a health condition that affects how your body turns food into energy. He can be treated with medicine given to him every day.

Mom gives Pumpy his medicine every morning and night and he starts to look stronger and healthier with each passing day.

Mom wants to take a trip from New Jersey, where she currently lives to Florida to visit her friends. Pumpy must travel with her so he can get his medicine every day. She looks on her laptop for a flight for the two of them and books it.

Upon their return home, Pumpy tells Oliver all about how exciting it was being under the seat of the plane. He smelled so many different smells and saw so many new things. He loved it. Oliver, just hearing this, is terrified and can't imagine leaving the house.

Mom's brother bought a house in Pennsylvania and she tells Pumpy that
he will go on a very long car ride with her to see the house. He's so
excited. Oliver hides behind the couch, hoping he will not be asked to go.

Pumpy has never seen such a big house. He explores giant rooms, one after another. There is a boy, named Julian, who lives there. He pets Pumpy and gives him treats. It's a wonderful time.

Again, Pumpy returns home. He's tired, so, after catching up on his sleep, he tells Oliver about his trip to Pennsylvania. Oliver hides his head under the blankets. He loves hearing the stories. Oliver starts to feel like he may be missing out. With Pumpy by his side, maybe some day he could join his family on their trips.

Oliver and Pumpy play together with their toys. They stretch in the sun.
They take their naps. Pumpy goes back to the vet. He is doing much better.

Mom and Ronnie decide they are going to take a trip to Los Angeles. Pumpy will go with them and he says, "See you soon, Oliver." Pumpy settles into his carrier for a six-hour flight. Mom booked a pet-friendly hotel so Pumpy can sleep there when she and Ronnie are out during the days.

Pumpy has a big hotel window. There he sits and watches robins and mockingbirds dance outside the window. It's a magnificent sight. When he gets tired, he plops down on the giant, king-sized bed.

Mom wants to take a trip to Greece with her friend, Tammy. She invites
Tammy over to the house to plan the flights and hotel. Oliver hears them
talking about Pumpy going away again with them. Tammy and Mom talk
about a Greek Island called Syros. This island is a cat sanctuary. Oliver
thinks surely that couldn't be scary. It's for cats. It's his time to try this.

The day they are to leave for Greece, Oliver gathers up all his courage. He crawls into the pet carrier that is by the front door meant for Pumpy. Mom sees Oliver in it and laughs. She says, "Oh Oliver, so you want to go this time, too?" surprisingly pleased.

Pumpy and Oliver are side by side, stored under seats on the plane. Pumpy reassures Oliver the entire time of what is going on.

They lounge in the hotel room while Tammy and Mom are touring Greece. They sit together in front of the large hotel window watching the herons and warblers tease them on the other side of the glass. They sleep on top of each other on one of the pillow-top beds.

On the third day of the trip,
harnesses are put on them and
they are shuffled off to a taxi. Then
they are placed on a boat. Pumpy
on Mom's lap and Oliver on
Tammy's lap. After a bit, they all step
out of the boat and onto the Island
of Syros. Oliver is not fearful but
excited. There are cats, like him,
running everywhere. It smells great.
He joins Pumpy and side by side
they explore the island together.

After a fun-filled trip, they are happy to return home. Oliver thinks to himself how grateful he is to have his stepbrother, Pumpy. They eat their pate cat food together and settle down for a long cat nap.

Annette is feeling very sad. She stares at a picture of Pumpkin and Oliver. They passed away a few years before. She misses her fuzzy friends. Becky from the animal rescue had dropped off a picture of herself holding a blue-eyed boy, named Lou. He needs a home. Becky told her that he would be a perfect new friend for Annette.

Annette and Ronnie go to meet Lou. They approach him slowly and he is so shy and timid. He sticks to the corner of the room. They know they must take him home. He will be showered with lots of love.

26

Lou hides under the bed, his wide eyes peering out.
He's scared but slowly inches forward.
He crawls into Annette's lap. He starts
making purring sounds. Annette and
Lou sleep side by side.

Lou and Annette go to the lake. Lou feels secure in his
backpack on Annette's back. They enjoy all that is around
them.

Lou and Annette go to the store to buy some food and the pate he loves. Lou always feels so safe in his backpack. He feels invincible.

Annette had planned a trip to Florida to enjoy the warmer weather. Off to the airport! With Lou in his backpack, they travel back and forth by plane.

Now it's time for the two of them to travel to visit Annette's father in Pennsylvania. Her dad is in a retirement home. He is so happy to see Lou. Lou licks his face and sits on his lap.

Once they are back at home, Lou seems lonely. Just as Pumpkin and Oliver had been there for each other, Lou needs a fuzzy stepbrother. Annette tells Lou he will have to share his food and toys but that she is sure he will like his new friend.

The next day, Annette goes to visit the owner of Rebecca's Rescues, Becky. She explains that Lou needs a friend.

Lou and Val are instantly friends. They are less than a year apart. They roll around together on the floor, jump and run together. They share their pate cat food nicely.

Lou and Val can't imagine life without each other. Lou is still shy but feels less timid with Val around. Lou still feels the most safe when he is in his backpack, though. There he thinks no one can touch him.

Annette, Lou, and Val are off to Grandma's house in Pennsylvania. The cats are excited. Annette has told them that Grandma loves birds. As they drive, they imagine chasing birds around the yard. Lou is in his backpack and Val is just on a leash as they drive.

Lou, on his hind legs, and Val, standing on a coffee can, they watch the birds in amazement. Birds of all colors and sizes fly around Grandma's house. She feeds them special seed that brings unusual birds. Later they will dream that they were chasing those birds.

Once they are back home again, Annette sits on the couch with Lou and Val. She thinks back to her first two cats, Pumpkin and Oliver. They were so similar to these two. One was shy and one outgoing. What can she do to help Lou feel more comfortable and leave his backpack behind? Annette says, "Ah, I know." She takes her laptop out and searches for cat island sanctuaries.

Lou barely fits in his backpack anymore. He peers up at Annette, anxious for what is to come. Val fights to get into his carrier. He is used to just being on a leash, but to go on a plane, he must get in the carrier. Finally, he relents and off they go to the airport.

The three of them sit at the airport terminal gate waiting for their flight to Maui, Lou in his backpack, Val in his carrier, and Annette between them. People smile at them and some ask cat-related questions. They get a lot of attention.

They arrive at the Lanai Cat Sanctuary, home to 700 rescued cats. Annette takes in the incredible number of cats on the large island of 4 acres. The cats there romp, play, and bask in the sun.

Lou stays in his backpack. Val prances back to Lou. He nudges the backpack over and puts his face in it. He rubs Lou's ear and waits for Lou to slowly put a paw out of the backpack. Then Lou sticks a leg out and then his entire body. He looks in awe at all the cats before him. Wow! They all look so happy. Lou thinks, "If Val is with me, then I can go look around some more." He feels all his shyness falling away. He feels free.

Annette and her daughter, Ronnie, help take care of a Momma cat that has just had five kittens. Ronnie has grown fond of one kitten in particular that is black with a white chin. She is going to keep that one and name her Alaska.

Ronnie and Alaska are inseparable. When Ronnie is home, Alaska sits in her lap and purrs. Alaska is a good communicator. She meows and meows. She grows quickly into a nice, big cat.

Alaska likes to drink only from the sink and enjoys cheese snacks. She is very shy when visitors come. She will hide under the blankets or the bed. She only seems to be comfortable with Ronnie.

Ronnie decides that maybe Alaska needs a fuzzy friend, a stepbrother. This might help her to be more outgoing with others. It had worked well with the other cats. She adopts an orange cat and names him Squash. Squash is a big, muscular cat.

Alaska smells Squash and
Squash licks her head. The
smell of Squash reminds
Alaska of her siblings she had
played with a while
back. She is excited. Squash
settles in nicely. They play,
nap, and eat together. They
enjoy hanging out on top of
the refrigerator.

Squash seems a little restless around the house, so Ronnie takes him on car rides. She doesn't need to put him in a crate. He is just fine on a leash. He sits with his paws on the car dashboard and looks at his surroundings with wide eyes. He loves adventure.

Ronnie and Squash get back home to find Alaska lounging in the bathroom sink. Ronnie wishes Alaska could be more adventurous like Squash. Alaska seems to just want to go under the covers whenever any visitors come over.

Annette comes over to visit and tells Ronnie about the cat island in Greece where Pumpkin and Oliver had the best time. She explains how much Val and Lou also loved the island in Hawaii too. Then she tells Ronnie about an island in Aosmina, Japan. Now this cat island is really special because cats outnumber humans there six to one! Ronnie says, "We must go together and take Squash and Alaska. This is just what Alaska needs."

Annette and Ronnie are at the airport with Squash on his leash and Alaska in her carrier. Travelers begin petting Squash and he purrs. Alaska backs up in her carrier, trying to not be seen.

They arrive in Japan and get on a ferry to go to the island. Squash is now sitting on top of Alaska's crate to get the best view of the sites. Ronnie feeds Alaska cheese snacks to keep her happy.

As they set foot on cat island in Aosmina, the cats run up to greet them. Squash meows with delight. He is so excited. He can't wait to explore. Alaska is not sure what to do, so Squash licks her head. He meows to her and turns his head to a high perch to the right. She follows him, trusting her step-brother. They jump up to a landing with a great view of the water. It looks like the same height as the refrigerator at home. Alaska likes it up there. She sees birds flying around her. She thinks she'd like to stay a while. This could be a lot of fun.

The End.

About the Author

Ronnie & our beloved Pumpkin

Annette & Shy Lou

Annette Morano has always been an avid animal lover. She has volunteered for Rebecca's Rescues for the past 14 years. She has fostered over 65 cats, from bottle babies to older cats in her own home until they were successfully adopted to their forever homes. She feels that we should all make time to volunteer because by giving back, you will then be blessed beyond your expectations. Thank you for supporting this book. The proceeds will help pay for the care of the cats in Rebecca's Rescues in Brick, NJ.